The Declaration of Independence - Explained

An Illustrated Book About the Origin of Our Nation

ISBN: 978-1-969705-01-4

Published by Crane Books - cranebooks.com

CRANE
BOOKS

The Declaration of Independence - Explained

An Illustrated Book About the Origin of Our Nation

Publisher:

Crane Books

cranebooks.com

Murrieta, California

ISBN 978-1-969705-01-4

Disclaimer:
Some illustrations in this book were created with the support of artificial intelligence (AI) tools. All graphics have been directed, edited, and finalized by the author and Crane Books illustration team to ensure historical and creative accuracy.

Library of Congress Cataloging-in-Publication Data

Vidal, Darryl, 1963–
The Declaration of Independence–Explained / Darryl Vidal.
p. cm.—(American History–Explained series)

Includes bibliographical references.

ISBN 978-1-969705-01-4 (pbk.)

1.   United States—History—Revolution, 1775–1783—Juvenile literature.

2.   United States—Politics and government—1775–1783—Juvenile literature.

3.   United States—Declaration of Independence—Juvenile literature.

4.   Jefferson, Thomas, 1743–1826—Juvenile literature.

      I. Title. II. Series: American History–Explained.

      Printed in the United States of America.

Introduction

When I was in college, I was challenged to memorize the Declaration of Independence by an acting teacher. The exercise was folly, but the lesson learned was that humans could memorize an amazing amount of information. It wasn't until then that I had ever read the Declaration. Of course, we'd studied it in High School American history but I'm not sure anyone really understood the importance of the action, the risks being taken or the utter severity of the situation in regards to the experiment known as the United States of America.

Although I wasn't able to complete the challenge, I did memorize the first and most of the second paragraph. Up to the line, "Life, Liberty and the Pursuit of Happiness." It has stayed with me still today.

As a father, I found myself wanting my children to understand more than just the words. I wanted them to feel the meaning behind the celebrations and ceremonies we often take for granted. On Memorial Day, Veterans Day, and especially on the Fourth of July, I reminded them that these were not just holidays on the calendar, they were remembrances of sacrifice, risk, and the courage of ordinary people who chose an extraordinary path.

The Declaration of Independence is not only a document of the past; it is the foundation of the freedoms we live with today. To grasp its importance, we have to place ourselves in the world of 1776. The American colonies were still deeply tied to Britain, dependent on its trade and under the weight of its taxes. Yet they had no voice in the laws that governed them.

As we step back in time, I want you to be able to relate to the events of the American Revolution as if it were happening today. What would it feel like if your parent's generation were almost all immigrants—from all over the globe, but in 1776, people in the United States' colonies had one thing in common, they were getting tired of the British control of their politics, laws and economics.

While the Crown insisted the American colonies would provide vast wealth for the empire, those of us who study this history can sense how differently the colonists themselves envisioned their future. Independence from the Crown was not a distant dream—it was becoming a necessity.

British soldiers patrolled the streets, while royal governors overruled colonial assemblies. To live under such constant authoritarianism was to feel both the weight of an empire and the stirrings of a people ready to risk everything for freedom.

The Risk of Revolution

The cry of "taxation without representation" was not a clever slogan—it was the lived reality of farmers, shopkeepers, and craftsmen who paid duties on sugar, stamps, and tea, all imposed by a distant Parliament in which no American had a seat. British imperial policy viewed the colonies as sources of revenue and raw materials, not as communities of free citizens. By the 1770s, resentment had hardened into resistance, and resistance into revolution.

But it was not only anger that fueled the decision to break away—it was an idea. The colonists were drawing on the bold political philosophy of the Enlightenment, a way of thinking that insisted all people had natural rights, given not by kings but by nature itself. Thinkers like John Locke had argued that government should exist only by the consent of the governed, and that when rulers became tyrants, the people had the right to alter or abolish that government.

Jefferson, Adams, Franklin, and the others gathered in Philadelphia knew the risk. By signing their names, they were not just declaring independence from Britain—they were declaring independence for the very concept of liberty itself. It was treason in the eyes of the Crown, but to them it was the beginning of a new nation.

The Danger of Treason

When the delegates of the Continental Congress gathered in Philadelphia, they knew exactly what was at stake. By drafting and signing the Declaration of Independence, they were committing what the British Crown defined as treason—the gravest of crimes. Treason was not punished with a fine or imprisonment; it was punished with death.

Hanging was the most common method, though some forms of execution were even more brutal. Each man who stepped forward to sign his name was placing his own life on the line, as well as his family's safety and fortune.

The delegates were not reckless rebels but men of property, education, and standing in their communities. Many were lawyers, merchants, or landowners with much to lose. By defying the King, they risked confiscation of their estates, destruction of their businesses, and even harm to their wives and children.

Benjamin Franklin, with his usual wit, summed up the gravity of their choice: "We must all hang together, or, most assuredly, we shall all hang separately." Behind the humor was a chilling truth—they were united by the real possibility of the gallows.

For some, the danger was even greater because they were well-known figures even across the Atlantic ocean. John Hancock, president of the Congress, deliberately signed his name in large, bold letters so the King could read it "without spectacles." His flourish was a direct challenge to British authority.

Others followed, not out of bravado, but out of duty. They believed that independence could not be secured by anonymous protest. It required visible, undeniable commitment. By signing, they transformed their cause from angry words into a binding promise of unity.

The courage of these men lay not in the absence of fear but in their willingness to face it. They accepted that their personal sacrifice might be the price of liberty for future generations. Every stroke of the pen was an act of defiance, but also an act of faith—that the idea of a free nation could outlast the danger to their own lives.

British Imperial Policy

When the first English colonies were established in North America in the early 1600s, Britain's imperial policy was loose and often inattentive. This "salutary neglect" allowed the colonies to govern themselves in many ways—passing local laws, running assemblies, and managing their own trade. For decades, the colonies thrived under this relative independence, developing unique economies and political cultures. Many colonists grew to see themselves not as dependents of the Crown, but as self-sufficient communities loyal to a distant king.

That balance began to change after the costly French and Indian War (1754–1763). Britain emerged victorious but deeply in debt, and Parliament turned to the colonies as a source of revenue. Taxes such as the Stamp Act and the Townshend Acts were designed to help cover war expenses and the cost of maintaining British troops in America. To colonists, however, these measures felt like an abrupt betrayal of the freedoms they had long enjoyed. What had once been an empire of mutual benefit now seemed like a system of extraction, where the colonies were treated as sources of money rather than partners in prosperity.

King George III, who had ascended to the throne in 1760, viewed the unrest across the Atlantic with suspicion and anger. To him, the colonists were not oppressed subjects but ungrateful children rebelling against lawful authority. He believed that yielding to their demands would weaken the empire and invite challenges from other colonies around the globe. By the mid-1770s, George dismissed their petitions and declared the colonies to be in open rebellion. For him, the revolution was not a political debate—it was treason. His determination to suppress it only deepened the resolve of the colonists to break free.

Taxation Without Representation

The phrase "taxation without representation" captured the frustration of colonists who were being taxed by a government in which they had no voice.

In the British system, laws were passed by Parliament, a body made up of representatives elected by the people of Britain. But the American colonies had no seats in Parliament, no elected officials to argue their case, and no vote in decisions that directly affected their daily lives.

When Parliament passed measures such as the Sugar Act of 1764 and the Stamp Act of 1765, colonists were expected to pay duties on everything from newspapers to legal documents, yet they had no way to influence those decisions. To them, this violated the basic principle that government should only levy taxes with the consent of the governed.

As the 1760s and 1770s unfolded, "no taxation without representation" became more than a complaint—it became a rallying cry. It was shouted in town meetings, written on protest pamphlets, and even painted on banners carried through colonial streets. Groups like the Sons of Liberty used it to unite merchants, artisans, and farmers under a common cause.

The slogan made the abstract issue of imperial power concrete and personal: every tax stamp purchased, every crate of taxed tea dumped into Boston Harbor, was proof that their rights were being ignored. By reducing a complex political struggle to a simple, memorable phrase, the colonists created a powerful tool of protest that gave their resistance energy and focus.

The Boston Tea Party - A Trigger Point for Revolution

By 1773, tensions between the colonies and Britain had been simmering for more than a decade. Taxes on paper, paint, glass, and especially tea had stirred outrage, but Parliament's decision to grant the East India Company a monopoly on tea imports struck a nerve. Colonists saw it not just as another tax, but as a direct attempt to undercut local merchants and force acceptance of taxation without representation.

On the night of December 16, 1773, a group of colonists disguised as Mohawk Indians boarded ships in Boston Harbor and dumped 342 chests of tea into the water. This bold act of defiance became known as the Boston Tea Party. It was more than vandalism—it was a symbolic rejection of British authority and a direct challenge to King George's rule.

The British response was swift and harsh. Parliament passed the Coercive Acts, which colonists dubbed the "Intolerable Acts." These laws closed Boston Harbor, restricted self-government, and placed Massachusetts under direct British control. Rather than intimidating the colonies, the measures united them. Colonists from

New York, Virginia, and beyond saw the punishment of Boston as a warning to all.

The Boston Tea Party, therefore, served as a trigger point. It transformed scattered resentment into collective resistance and pushed the colonies closer to declaring independence. It showed Britain that the colonists were willing to risk everything—even war—to defend their rights.

Enlightenment Philosophy

The Enlightenment, often called the "Age of Reason," was a movement in the 17th and 18th centuries that placed human reason, science, and individual rights above tradition and unquestioned authority. Thinkers like John Locke, Montesquieu, and Rousseau challenged the idea that kings ruled by divine right and instead argued that government should exist only to serve the people.

These ideas reached across the Atlantic, where colonial leaders studied them closely. In America, the Enlightenment inspired a belief that all men were born with "natural rights" that no monarch could take away. For the colonists, Enlightenment thought gave intellectual and moral weight to the idea of independence. It told them they weren't just rebelling; they were asserting timeless principles of justice.

Adam Smith, a Scottish philosopher and economist, became one of the most influential figures of the Enlightenment with the publication of The Wealth of Nations in 1776—the very same year the American colonies declared independence. Smith argued that economies function best when individuals are free to pursue their own interests within open markets, guided not by government micromanagement but by what he famously called the "invisible hand" of competition and exchange.

His vision challenged the old mercantilist system, in which colonies existed primarily to enrich their mother country through strict trade controls and heavy taxation. Instead, Smith suggested that prosperity arose when nations allowed trade to flow freely and when governments limited their interference to protecting property rights and enforcing justice.

Ideas That Shaped Independence

John Locke
Natural Rights –
Life, Liberty, Property

Montesquieu
Separation of Powers
Balanced Government

Jean-Jacquesuu
Power from the People

Social Contract
Power from the People

Adam Smith
Free Markets

For American leaders, Smith's ideas provided both validation and ammunition. Colonists had long bristled at Britain's mercantilist policies—laws that restricted whom they could trade with and funneled profits back to England. Smith's work confirmed what many colonists already believed: that Britain's economic control was stifling rather than strengthening them. In the grand debate over independence, Smith's emphasis on free markets and limited government power dovetailed with Jefferson's and Franklin's embrace of natural rights and liberty.

Together, these ideas created a political philosophy that shaped not only the Declaration of Independence but also the economic foundation of the new United States. Smith did not write with America specifically in mind, but his Enlightenment theories became part of the intellectual fuel that justified breaking away from Britain and building a republic where economic freedom was considered as essential as political freedom.

In Britain, Enlightenment philosophy had a more complicated effect. Many in Parliament and among the educated classes embraced new ideas about economics, science, and government reform. Thinkers like Adam Smith and David Hume were reshaping British views on commerce and society.

Yet when it came to the colonies, the government often clung to older notions of imperial control and loyalty to the Crown. This created a striking contrast: while colonists were using Enlightenment arguments to demand self-government, many British leaders saw those same arguments as dangerous challenges to stability and authority.

To them, philosophy was welcome in the lecture hall but threatening when applied to colonial resistance. The divergence revealed a critical tension—Enlightenment ideals were spreading everywhere, but in America they were being turned into a revolutionary blueprint.

Chapter 1: "When in the Course of Human Events…"

"WHEN in the Course of human Events, it becomes necessary for one People to dissolve the Political Bands which have connected them with another, and to assume among the Powers of the Earth, the separate and equal Station to which the Laws of Nature and of Nature's God entitle them, a decent Respect to the Opinions of Mankind requires that they should declare the causes which impel them to the Separation."

The Declaration of Independence begins with words that sound almost timeless: "When in the course of human events…" This opening does not rush to anger or accusation. Instead, it sets a calm and deliberate tone, as if the authors were stating a universal truth rather than a temporary grievance. By speaking in broad, philosophical language, Thomas Jefferson and the Continental Congress elevated the colonial struggle beyond a local dispute with Britain and placed it in the context of humanity's larger story.

The phrase announces that what follows is not an impulsive rebellion but a reasoned decision. The colonists present themselves as participants in the "course of human events," suggesting that their actions are part of the natural unfolding of history. They imply that just as peoples before them have risen, separated, and claimed their rights, so too do the American colonies now step onto the stage of nations.

This opening was crucial because it framed the Declaration as more than a quarrel with King George III. It invited the world to view the American Revolution as a legitimate, even inevitable, step in human progress. By beginning this way, the founders claimed moral and philosophical ground that made their break from Britain not only justifiable but also dignified in the eyes of other nations.

The Necessity of Separation

The opening sentence continues: "…it becomes necessary for one people to dissolve the political bands which have connected them with another, and to assume among the powers of the earth, the separate and equal station to which the Laws of Nature and of Nature's God entitle them…"

This phrase lays out both the cause and the justification for independence. First, Jefferson acknowledges the necessity of separation—not as a rash choice, but as something compelled by circumstance. The words "it becomes necessary" signal that the colonies are acting out of duty, not desire. They are not abandoning Britain out of impatience or pride; they are answering an unavoidable historical moment.

Second, the sentence introduces the principle of equality among nations. By claiming a "separate and equal station among the powers of the earth," the colonies assert that they have the same right to sovereignty as any kingdom or state in Europe. This was a radical step—thirteen small colonies declaring themselves the peers of ancient monarchies like France and Spain.

Finally, Jefferson invokes the "Laws of Nature and of Nature's God." This appeal tied their political claim to Enlightenment philosophy. Thinkers like Locke and Rousseau argued that rights do not come from kings but from nature itself, and therefore from God who authored nature. By rooting their cause in universal law, not just English law, the colonists positioned their struggle as morally sound and universally valid.

This single sentence accomplishes much: it presents the break with Britain as reluctant but required, asserts equality with other nations, and grounds the argument in natural law. Before the Declaration ever accuses King George of tyranny, it has already justified America's place among free nations.

Chapter 2: "We Hold These Truths to Be Self-Evident" (The Core Principles)

"We hold these Truths to be self-evident, that all Men are created equal, that they are endowed by their Creator with certain unalienable Rights, that among these are Life, Liberty, and the Pursuit of Happiness"

The Preamble is often regarded as the philosophical heart of the Declaration. In just a few sentences, it condenses Enlightenment principles into a powerful argument for liberty.

"We hold these truths to be self-evident…"

Jefferson begins with the language of universal truth. By calling these principles "self-evident," he suggests they are so clear that they require no proof. This rhetorical move strips away the need for debate: the truths are assumed as natural, not man-made.

"…that all men are created equal…"

This is the most famous phrase, asserting a radical equality before law and morality. At the time, equality did not mean identical social standing or wealth, but rather that no person was born with a natural right to rule over another. It struck directly at the heart of monarchy and inherited privilege.

"…that they are endowed by their Creator with certain unalienable Rights…"

Here Jefferson links natural rights to divine authority. Rights are not gifts from governments; they are inherent in human existence. By using "unalienable," he stresses that these rights cannot be surrendered or taken away.

"…that among these are Life, Liberty, and the pursuit of Happiness."

Borrowed and adapted from John Locke's "life, liberty, and property," Jefferson's phrase expands the scope. By replacing "property" with "pursuit of happiness," he elevates the idea beyond material possessions to a more universal aspiration: the right to seek fulfillment and well-being.

"That to secure these rights, Governments are instituted among Men, deriving their just powers from the consent of the governed…"

This statement defines the purpose of government: not to grant rights, but to protect them. It also establishes the source of legitimate power—the people. This is Rousseau's social contract in plain form.

"That whenever any Form of Government becomes destructive of these ends, it is the Right of the People to alter or to abolish it, and to institute new Government…"

Here lies the revolutionary core. If a government fails in its duty, the people not only may replace it, they ought to. Jefferson defines revolution not as rebellion but as a rational correction when government betrays its purpose.

Why the Preamble Matters

The Preamble does more than introduce grievances—it provides a philosophical blueprint for democracy. It rejects monarchy, affirms natural rights, defines government as a protector of those rights, and asserts the people's ultimate sovereignty. Later revolutions in France, Latin America, and even modern civil rights movements would echo its language and ideals.

All Men are Create Equal

The declaration that "all men are created equal" was revolutionary in 1776. At its core, it drew from Enlightenment philosophy, particularly John Locke's belief in natural rights. By proclaiming equality at birth, Jefferson rejected the long-standing idea that kings and aristocrats were divinely appointed to rule over others.

Though the words did not erase slavery, inequality, or injustice at the time, they established a moral foundation that future generations would invoke in the struggle for civil rights and human dignity.

Life, Liberty and the Pursuit of Happiness

When Jefferson wrote that all men are "endowed by their Creator with certain unalienable Rights… among these are Life, Liberty, and the pursuit of Happiness," he was drawing directly from the Enlightenment tradition. John Locke, in his Second Treatise of Government (1689), had defined natural rights as "life, liberty, and property." Locke's formulation emphasized the protection of personal safety, individual freedom, and ownership of possessions as the basis of civil society. For Locke, property was not only land or goods but also the fruit of one's labor, something that government was bound to safeguard.

Jefferson, however, chose to alter the third element. By replacing "property" with the "pursuit of happiness," he broadened the concept from material security to a more universal human aspiration. The phrase captured the idea that individuals have the right to seek fulfillment, self-improvement, and well-being in whatever way their conscience and talents lead them—so long as it does not infringe on the rights of others. This shift gave the Declaration a more moral and aspirational tone, resonating not only with landowners but with all who sought freedom and opportunity.

The change also carried political weight. Jefferson knew that grounding liberty solely in property rights might limit the Declaration's reach and reduce its moral power. By elevating "happiness" as a natural right, the colonies' cause appeared not merely as a defense of economic interests, but as a defense of human dignity itself. It allowed the Declaration to speak in universal terms, giving it lasting influence well beyond 1776.

The Consent of the Governed

One of the most radical claims in the Declaration of Independence is that "Governments are instituted among Men, deriving their just powers from the consent of the governed. That whenever any Form of Government becomes destructive of these ends, it is the Right of the People to alter or abolish it…"

This principle shattered the traditional foundations of monarchy. In Europe, kings often ruled by divine right, claiming authority came directly from God. Jefferson and the Continental Congress rejected this outright. Legitimate government, they declared, does not come from heaven or hereditary power—it comes from the will of the people.

The idea of consent of the governed is at the core of the social contract theory advanced by Enlightenment thinkers like John Locke and Jean-Jacques Rousseau. According to Locke, people leave the state of nature and form governments not to surrender their rights, but to secure them more effectively.

When rulers protect life, liberty, and property, they retain authority; when they violate these rights, they lose their legitimacy. Rousseau went further, emphasizing that political authority must always reflect the "general will" of the people. Jefferson distilled these philosophies into a single revolutionary principle: the people are sovereign, and their consent is the only true source of political power.

The second half of the statement carries profound implications: if a government fails in its duty, the people may alter it—through reform, elections, or constitutional change—or, if necessary, abolish it altogether. In 1776, this was nothing short of treason against Britain.

Yet it also established a framework that outlived the Revolution. Americans later invoked this principle in movements for abolition, women's suffrage, civil rights, and beyond. Each time, reformers pointed back to the Declaration to argue that government had strayed from its purpose and required correction.

Thus, Jefferson gave future generations both a warning and a promise: governments exist only by the people's consent, and whenever power is abused, the right to resist and rebuild belongs not to kings, but to the people themselves.

Prudence and the Case for Revolution

In this segment, Jefferson acknowledges a crucial principle: change should not come lightly. "Prudence, indeed, will dictate that Governments long established should not be changed for light and transient causes." By beginning here, the Declaration dismisses any notion that the colonies are reckless or impatient. History shows, Jefferson writes, that people are generally more inclined to endure injustice than to risk upheaval. This point establishes the colonists as reluctant revolutionaries—men who tolerated abuses until those abuses became intolerable.

The tone then shifts: when a government engages in a "long train of abuses and usurpations" aimed at imposing despotism, revolution becomes not only a right but a duty. This is Jefferson's moral pivot. He argues that the colonies have endured enough, and that self-preservation now demands resistance. The choice is no longer between loyalty and rebellion, but between slavery and freedom.

Finally, Jefferson frames the colonies' struggle in universal terms: their patience has been tested, their rights trampled, and necessity now compels them to act. The charges against King George III are not vague or emotional; they are presented as evidence of tyranny to be laid before the "candid world." By ending this paragraph with a transition to "Facts," Jefferson signals that the Declaration will move from philosophy to indictment, blending moral reasoning with concrete proof.

This passage is important because it balances restraint with urgency: the colonists are not anarchists seeking chaos, but rational people forced into revolution by a consistent pattern of oppression.

Chapter 3: "He Has…" (The Grievances Against the King)

"He has refused his Assent to Laws, the most wholesome and necessary for the public Good."

The Grievances in Context

The middle of the Declaration of Independence presents a long list of accusations against King George III—twenty-seven in total. To the casual reader, they might seem like a jumble of complaints, but Jefferson and the Continental Congress organized them with purpose. These grievances can be understood in five major categories: political interference, judicial abuses, military oppression, economic and trade restrictions, and the deliberate incitement of violence and division. Together, they formed a portrait of a king who had abandoned his role as protector and instead acted as a tyrant.

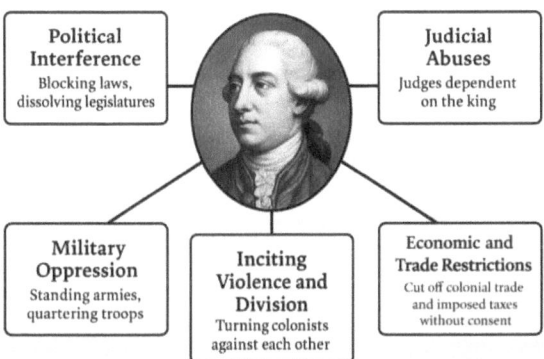

GRIEVANCES AGAINST KING GEORGE III

Political Interference
Blocking laws, dissolving legislatures

Judicial Abuses
Judges dependent on the king

Military Oppression
Standing armies, quartering troops

Inciting Violence and Division
Turning colonists against each other

Economic and Trade Restrictions
Cut off colonial trade and imposed taxes without consent

Political Interference

At the heart of the colonists' frustrations was the King's direct interference in their political life. He blocked laws that were necessary for the colonies' growth and well-being, dissolved legislatures that resisted his will, and left entire regions unrepresented by refusing to hold new elections.

These actions stripped the colonies of the right to govern themselves, making clear that self-rule was impossible under British oversight. Political institutions that should have reflected the will of the people became tools of royal dominion.

Judicial Abuses

The colonists also charged the King with corrupting justice. Judges no longer held independent positions, but served at the King's pleasure, reliant on him for their salaries and tenure. Trial by jury, a right cherished in English law, was repeatedly denied. Colonists could even be shipped across the ocean to face trial in Britain for alleged crimes, making fair judgment nearly impossible. Through these abuses, justice—meant to be impartial—was turned into an instrument of intimidation.

Military Oppression

Equally alarming was the use of military force to enforce obedience. British standing armies occupied the colonies during peacetime without consent, and their authority was placed above that of civil institutions. Colonists were compelled to house troops in their own homes, a practice that bred resentment and fear. Worse still, soldiers accused of crimes against colonists were often shielded from punishment through sham trials. Rather than protecting the people, the King's armies became symbols of oppression.

Economic and Trade Restrictions

The economic life of the colonies was also targeted. The King cut off colonial trade with the wider world and imposed taxes without consent, stripping the colonists of both prosperity and political voice. These restrictions demonstrated that Britain viewed the colonies not as partners, but as sources of revenue to be controlled and exploited. Economic oppression reinforced the sense that liberty was impossible under a system that denied the colonists control over their livelihoods.

Inciting Violence and Division

Perhaps most shocking were the charges that the King deliberately unleashed violence. He was accused of burning towns, plundering coasts, hiring foreign mercenaries, and declaring war on his own subjects. Colonists were forced into combat against their will, enslaved people were encouraged to rebel, and Native tribes were incited to attack frontier settlements. These actions revealed a ruler willing to destroy his own people rather than respect their rights. It was the ultimate proof that the King sought not reconciliation, but absolute tyranny.

Chapter 4: "For Quartering Large Bodies of Armed Troops…" (The Pretended Legislation)

"For quartering large Bodies of Armed Troops among us."

Among the grievances Jefferson called "pretended legislation" were the most despised acts ever imposed on the colonies—laws forced upon them without consent. At the heart of this accusation were the Intolerable Acts of 1774, Britain's harsh response to the Boston Tea Party.

These laws closed Boston Harbor, restricted town meetings, placed Massachusetts under military rule, and required colonists to provide housing and supplies for British soldiers.

Quartering of Armed Troops

The Quartering Act in particular outraged Americans, as it forced families to bear the cost and burden of maintaining an occupying army in their own communities. To colonists, this was not the behavior of a protector, but of a conqueror.

Colonists deeply resented the quartering of British troops, seeing it as both an invasion of privacy and a symbol of tyranny. Having soldiers forced into their homes disrupted family life, strained already scarce resources, and created daily tension between civilians and the occupying army. Beyond the practical burdens, quartering was viewed as proof that Britain no longer saw the colonies as loyal subjects but as enemies to be subdued. To many, it represented the loss of liberty itself—if the government could send soldiers to live in one's home without consent, then no right or boundary was truly secure. This resentment became one of the most powerful motivators for independence, later enshrined in the Third Amendment of the U.S. Constitution, which forbids such practices.

Taxation Without Consent

Equally offensive were the taxes Parliament imposed without colonial representation. The Stamp Act, the Townshend Acts, and the Tea Act were all seen as violations of the principle of self-government. Colonists argued that taxation without consent was theft, and each new law reinforced their belief that Britain intended to reduce them to subjects rather than partners. By labeling these measures "pretended legislation," Jefferson suggested that such laws held no legitimacy because they were enacted without the consent of the governed.

Trials Overseas

Another abuse was the Crown's practice of sending colonists abroad for trial. Under the guise of justice, accused colonists could be transported to England or placed under admiralty courts, where juries were absent and outcomes often predetermined. This denied them the rights guaranteed to Englishmen and made justice a weapon of intimidation.

Together, these measures formed the legal foundation of the colonists' case for independence. Britain had not merely violated their rights; it had imposed laws designed to control, punish, and subdue.

By cataloging these acts as "pretended legislation," the Declaration presented independence as a matter of law as well as principle. If government derives its authority from the consent of the governed, then the King's laws, forced without consent, were void— and the people were justified in creating a new system to secure their liberties.

Chapter 5: "In Every Stage of These Oppressions…" (The Failed Appeals)

"In every stage of these Oppressions we have Petitioned for Redress in the most humble Terms: Our repeated Petitions have been answered only by repeated Injury. A Prince, whose Character is thus marked by every act which may define a Tyrant, is unfit to be the Ruler of a free People."

The colonists were not quick to rebellion. For years before independence was declared, they wrote letters, sent delegations, and pleaded with the Crown to reconsider its policies. These petitions were often written with great respect, even humility, affirming loyalty to the King while asking for relief from unfair taxes, unjust laws, and military occupation.

The Olive Branch Petition of 1775 is one of the clearest examples, in which the Second Continental Congress begged King George III to find a peaceful solution. Instead of being heard, their appeals were ignored or met with harsher measures. This constant dismissal left many colonists feeling that peaceful negotiation was no longer possible.

Jefferson's words—"answered only by repeated injury"—speak to the bitterness of that disappointment. Every time colonists extended an olive branch, they found the hand that reached back carried chains, not compromise.

By 1776, it had become clear that the Crown would not treat the colonies as equal partners but as subjects to be controlled. The King's refusal to even acknowledge their petitions revealed the deep rift between the empire's vision of obedience and the colonies' growing demand for liberty.

This passage then delivers its sharpest blow: calling the King a "Tyrant." For Jefferson and his fellow delegates, this was not just an insult—it was a legal and moral declaration. A ruler who repeatedly ignores the voice of his people and answers their pleas with punishment has broken the fundamental contract of government.

By branding King George III as a tyrant, the Declaration justified not only resistance but the complete severing of political ties. It proclaimed to the world that a free people could no longer be ruled by a monarch who refused to hear them, and that the colonies had no choice but to govern themselves.

Chapter 6: "Nor have we been wanting in Attentions to our British Brethren."

"Nor have we been wanting in Attentions to our British Brethren. We have warned them from Time to Time of Attempts by their Legislature to extend an unwarrantable Jurisdiction over us. We have reminded them of the Circumstances of our Emigration and Settlement here."

One of the most striking aspects of the Declaration is that the colonists did not frame their quarrel as being with *all* of Britain, but specifically with its rulers. In this passage, Jefferson emphasizes that Americans had not ignored their "British brethren." They had written to the people of England directly, reminding them that colonists were once their neighbors, bound by blood, culture, and shared history.

They pointed out that the colonies had been founded by English settlers who sought opportunity and liberty, and who had carried with them the customs and laws of their homeland. The Revolution was not meant to erase this kinship; rather, it was an effort to preserve the very rights that Englishmen themselves valued.

Despite these appeals, the colonists received no support from ordinary Britons. The people of England, too, had turned a deaf ear. Jefferson suggests that the colonists had tried every possible form of persuasion—warning, reminding, appealing to justice, even invoking the bonds of family—and yet the response was silence.

In that silence lay a painful realization: the mother country no longer regarded the colonies as brothers, but as subordinates whose protests could be ignored. This rejection deepened the sense of isolation felt in America and made independence not just a political necessity but an emotional break as well.

The closing lines are both resolute and conciliatory. If Britain will not stand with the colonies, then they must accept separation and treat Britain as they would any other nation. "Enemies in war, in peace, friends" became the guiding principle. The colonies would not seek endless hatred, but they could no longer afford to be bound by false loyalty.

This statement gave the struggle a moral clarity: America had exhausted every effort to preserve ties peacefully and now must face the unavoidable reality of standing apart. It is an acknowledgment of loss, but also a vision of hope—that one day, peace and friendship might replace conflict, once independence was secured.

Chapter 7: "We, Therefore, the Representatives…" (The Bold Declaration)

"We, therefore, the Representatives of the UNITED STATES OF AMERICA, in General Congress, Assembled, appealing to the Supreme Judge of the World for the Rectitude of our Intentions, do, in the Name, and by Authority of the good People of these Colonies, solemnly Publish and Declare, That these United Colonies are, and of Right ought to be, Free and Independent States; that they are absolved from all Allegiance to the British Crown…And for the support of this Declaration, with a firm Reliance on the Protection of divine Providence, we mutually pledge to each other our Lives, our Fortunes, and our sacred Honor."

And so, the representatives of the thirteen colonies, gathered in Congress, declared to the world what had long been building in their hearts. With full faith that their cause was just, and with an appeal to the highest authority of all, they announced that these colonies were now—and by every principle of right ought to be— free and independent states.

No longer would they owe allegiance to the British Crown, nor be bound by its laws or decrees. The ties of empire were cut, and in their place stood a new nation, able to wage war, make peace, build alliances, and trade as equals among the powers of the earth.

This was not a declaration made lightly, nor by men seeking personal gain. It was sealed with a pledge: their lives, their fortunes, and their sacred honor. Each man who signed knew that failure would mean ruin—death for treason, confiscation of property, and disgrace upon his family. Yet they pledged it all, not for themselves alone, but for the generations to come.

With these words, the American colonies stepped fully into history. They had not only broken away from Britain; they had embraced the identity of a free people, bound together by shared sacrifice and unshakable resolve. The Declaration of Independence was more than a document—it was a promise, forged in courage, that liberty would be the foundation of a new nation.

When I first encountered the words of the Declaration, I was too young to feel the full weight of what they meant. Only later did I realize that behind the grand language stood men who risked everything, and a people who stepped into the unknown with courage as their only guarantee. They did not know if the experiment would succeed. They only knew that liberty was worth the risk.

Chapter 8: The Legacy of 1776

The Declaration of Independence did not end with the Revolution. Its words, especially Jefferson's statement that "all men are created equal," echoed through American history as a challenge to each new generation. The Revolution secured freedom from Britain, but the promise of liberty and equality was far from complete. From that moment on, the Declaration became both a foundation and a measuring stick for the nation's progress.

In the early 1800s, abolitionists seized upon the Declaration's language to argue against slavery. Leaders such as Frederick Douglass pointed out the contradiction between a nation built on liberty and the continued enslavement of millions. Douglass's famous question—"What, to the American slave, is your Fourth of July?"—reminded Americans that the ideals of 1776 remained unfinished business. The Civil War and President Abraham Lincoln's Emancipation Proclamation drew directly on the Declaration's promise, as Lincoln called it a "rebirth of freedom" to make the nation live up to its founding principles.

The struggle continued into the 20th century with the Civil Rights Movement. Martin Luther King Jr. invoked the Declaration in his I Have a Dream speech, describing it as a "promissory note" that America had yet to honor for all its citizens. Women's rights activists, too, borrowed the Declaration's form and language in the 1848 Declaration of Sentiments, demanding equality for women in the same spirit as Jefferson's call for independence. Each of these movements drew strength and legitimacy from the vision of 1776.

The legacy of the Declaration is not that it solved every problem of freedom, but that it gave Americans a common text to return to when justice seemed out of reach. Its words remind us that liberty is not a finished achievement but a continuing effort. The founders pledged their "lives, fortunes, and sacred honor" to begin that effort. It is up to every generation to carry it forward.

As I've studied and reflected on this moment in history, I've come to see the Declaration not as a relic behind glass, but as a living challenge. It calls each of us to remember that freedom is fragile, that it must be protected, and that it always requires sacrifice. The men who pledged their lives, fortunes, and sacred honor could not imagine the world we live in today, but they trusted that future generations would inherit the responsibility of preserving what they began.

And so, as we close this book, I hope you will carry forward not just the story of July 4, 1776, but the spirit of it. The courage of the founders is not locked in the past—it is a reminder for us, here and now, that freedom endures when ordinary people choose to defend it with extraordinary resolve. To all of you reading this: you are the next generation. The story of the Declaration of Independence is not only about what happened long ago—it's about what can still happen when people choose courage over fear. The founders risked everything so that freedom could have a chance. My hope is that you understand the weight of their sacrifice and the meaning of their words.

What you do with that knowledge matters. You may not face the same dangers they did, but you will face choices that test your integrity, your honor, and your sense of responsibility. May you choose wisely. May you value liberty. And may you carry forward the promise of 1776 into your own time.

The Legacy of 1776 - the Enduring Fight for Freedom

1776 — The Declaration of Independence
The Continental Congress signs the Declaration of Independence

1861 — The Civil War
The fight to end slavery reaches its climax. Lincoln frames the war as a struggle to fulfill the promises of the Declaration.

1863 — Emancipation Proclamation
Lincoln issues the proclamation declaring enslaved people in Confederate states free.

1865 — The 13th Amendment
Slavery is officially abolished in the United States.

1920 — Women's Suffrage Movement
Women's Suffrage Movement Beginning with the Seneca Falls Convention women demand the right to vote

1930 — Unionization and Labor Rights
Workers organize to demand safer conditions, fair pay, and the right to unionize

1960's — Civil Rights Movement
African Americans and allies struggle to end segregation and gain equal rights under the law.

1963 — Martin Luther King Jr.
"I Have a Dream" King calls the Declaration a "promissory note" to all Americans

John F. Kennedy assassinated
President Kennedy's vision of civil rights and a "New Frontier" is cut short

1968 — RFK & MLK Jr. assassinated
Two major voices for justice are silenced, intensifying unrest

1989 — Fall of the Berlin Wall
The Cold War ends, symbolizing the triumph of democratic ideals over authoritarian control

2001 — September 11 Attacks
September 11 Attacks A new era of conflict begins, with struggles balancing liberty and security

2020 — Renewed Struggles for Free Speech and Civil Liberties
Movements across the political spectrum debate what freedom means in a digital, divided world.

2025 — Shooting of Charlie Kirk
The attack on a modern political leader highlights ongoing tensions in America's democratic life and the enduring challenge of protecting both freedom and safety.

The Complete Text

WHEN in the Course of human Events, it becomes necessary for one People to dissolve the Political Bands which have connected them with another, and to assume among the Powers of the Earth, the separate and equal Station to which the Laws of Nature and of Nature's God entitle them, a decent Respect to the Opinions of Mankind requires that they should declare the causes which impel them to the Separation.

We hold these Truths to be self-evident, that all Men are created equal, that they are endowed by their Creator with certain unalienable Rights, that among these are Life, Liberty, and the Pursuit of Happiness—That to secure these Rights, Governments are instituted among Men, deriving their just Powers from the Consent of the Governed, that whenever any Form of Government becomes destructive of these Ends, it is the Right of the People to alter or to abolish it, and to institute new Government, laying its Foundation on such Principles, and organizing its Powers in such Form, as to them shall seem most likely to effect their Safety and Happiness. Prudence, indeed, will dictate that Governments long established should not be changed for light and transient Causes; and accordingly all Experience hath shewn, that Mankind are more disposed to suffer, while Evils are sufferable, than to right themselves by abolishing the Forms to which they are accustomed. But when a long Train of Abuses and Usurpations, pursuing invariably the same Object, evinces a Design to reduce them under absolute Despotism, it is their Right, it is their Duty, to throw off such Government, and to provide new Guards for their future Security. Such has been the patient Sufferance of these Colonies; and such is now the Necessity which constrains them to alter their former Systems of Government. The History of the present King of Great-Britain is a History of repeated Injuries and Usurpations, all having in direct Object the Establishment of an absolute Tyranny over these States. To prove this, let Facts be submitted to a candid World.

He has refused his Assent to Laws, the most wholesome and necessary for the public Good.

He has forbidden his Governors to pass Laws of immediate and pressing Importance, unless suspended in their Operation till his Assent should be obtained; and when so suspended, he has utterly neglected to attend to them.

He has refused to pass other Laws for the Accommodation of large Districts of People, unless those People would relinquish the Right of Representation in the Legislature, a Right inestimable to them, and formidable to Tyrants only.

He has called together Legislative Bodies at Places unusual, uncomfortable, and distant from the Depository of their public Records, for the sole Purpose of fatiguing them into Compliance with his Measures.

He has dissolved Representative Houses repeatedly, for opposing with manly Firmness his Invasions on the Rights of the People.

He has refused for a long Time, after such Dissolutions, to cause others to be elected; whereby the Legislative Powers, incapable of Annihilation, have returned to the People at large for their exercise; the State remaining in the mean time exposed to all the Dangers of Invasion from without, and Convulsions within.

He has endeavoured to prevent the Population of these States; for that Purpose obstructing the Laws for Naturalization of Foreigners; refusing to pass others to encourage their Migrations hither, and raising the Conditions of new Appropriations of Lands.

He has obstructed the Administration of Justice, by refusing his Assent to Laws for establishing Judiciary Powers.

He has made Judges dependent on his Will alone, for the Tenure of their Offices, and the Amount and Payment of their Salaries.

He has erected a Multitude of new Offices, and sent hither Swarms of Officers to harass our People, and eat out their Substance.

He has kept among us, in Times of Peace, Standing Armies, without the consent of our Legislatures.

He has affected to render the Military independent of and superior to the Civil Power.

He has combined with others to subject us to a Jurisdiction foreign to our Constitution, and unacknowledged by our Laws; giving his Assent to their Acts of pretended Legislation:

For quartering large Bodies of Armed Troops among us:

For protecting them, by a mock Trial, from Punishment for any Murders which they should commit on the Inhabitants of these States:

For cutting off our Trade with all Parts of the World:

For imposing Taxes on us without our Consent:

For depriving us, in many Cases, of the Benefits of Trial by Jury:

For transporting us beyond Seas to be tried for pretended Offences:

For abolishing the free System of English Laws in a neighbouring Province, establishing therein an arbitrary Government, and enlarging its Boundaries, so as to render it at once an Example and fit Instrument for introducing the same absolute Rule into these Colonies:

For taking away our Charters, abolishing our most valuable Laws, and altering fundamentally the Forms of our Governments:

For suspending our own Legislatures, and declaring themselves invested with Power to legislate for us in all Cases whatsoever.

He has abdicated Government here, by declaring us out of his Protection and waging War against us.

He has plundered our Seas, ravaged our Coasts, burnt our Towns, and destroyed the Lives of our People.

He is, at this Time, transporting large Armies of foreign Mercenaries to compleat the Works of Death, Desolation, and Tyranny, already begun with circumstances of Cruelty and Perfidy, scarcely paralleled in the most barbarous Ages, and totally unworthy the Head of a civilized Nation.

He has constrained our fellow Citizens taken Captive on the high Seas to bear Arms against their Country, to become the Executioners of their Friends and Brethren, or to fall themselves by their Hands.

He has excited domestic Insurrections amongst us, and has endeavoured to bring on the Inhabitants of our Frontiers, the merciless Indian Savages, whose known Rule of Warfare, is an undistinguished Destruction, of all Ages, Sexes and Conditions.

In every stage of these Oppressions we have Petitioned for Redress in the most humble Terms: Our repeated Petitions have been answered only by repeated Injury. A Prince, whose Character is thus marked by every act which may define a Tyrant, is unfit to be the Ruler of a free People.

Nor have we been wanting in Attentions to our British Brethren. We have warned them from Time to Time of Attempts by their Legislature to extend an unwarrantable Jurisdiction over us. We have reminded them of the Circumstances of our Emigration and Settlement here. We have appealed to their native Justice and Magnanimity, and we have conjured them by the

Ties of our common Kindred to disavow these Usurpations, which, would inevitably interrupt our Connections and Correspondence. They too have been deaf to the Voice of Justice and of Consanguinity. We must, therefore, acquiesce in the Necessity, which denounces our Separation, and hold them, as we hold the rest of Mankind, Enemies in War, in Peace, Friends.

We, therefore, the Representatives of the UNITED STATES OF AMERICA, in General Congress, Assembled, appealing to the Supreme Judge of the World for the Rectitude of our Intentions, do, in the Name, and by Authority of the good People of these Colonies, solemnly Publish and Declare, That these United Colonies are, and of Right ought to be, Free and Independent States; that they are absolved from all Allegiance to the British Crown, and that all political Connection between them and the State of Great-Britain, is and ought to be totally dissolved; and that as Free and Independent States, they have full Power to levy War, conclude Peace, contract Alliances, establish Commerce, and to do all other Acts and Things which Independent States may of right do. And for the support of this Declaration, with a firm Reliance on the Protection of divine Providence, we mutually pledge to each other our Lives, our Fortunes, and our sacred Honor.

Signed by Order and in Behalf of the Congress,

JOHN HANCOCK, President.

Attest.

CHARLES THOMSON, Secretary.

Dedication

To the Class of 2030—

May you learn the truth about the fight for freedom and the courage it takes to stand against tyranny. May you grow wise enough to recognize those who do not have your best interests at heart, and strong enough to protect the liberty entrusted to you. The story of 1776 is not only our past—it is your inheritance and your responsibility for the future.